WEST WITH LEWIS AND CLARK

The Story of the Corps of Discovery

An Activity Book for Children

Written & illustrated by William E. & Jan C. Hill

© Copyright HillHouse, 2000

The purchaser of this activity book may reproduce individual pages or activities for use only in his/her own classroom. However, permission is not granted for use within the entire school. The reproduction of the entire book for use within a school or district is strictly prohibited.

All rights reserved. This book, or any parts thereof, may not be reproduced in any manner, other than that described above, without the written permission of the authors/publisher. HillHouse, 91 Wood Road, Centereach, New York 11720-1619.

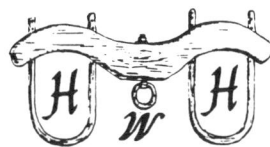

Printing 5 4
2009

ISBN 0-9636071-4-6
hillhousew@aol.com
www.hillhousew.com

WEST WITH LEWIS AND CLARK

The story of Lewis and Clark and the Corps of Discovery is one of the greatest stories in American History. It began when President Thomas Jefferson purchased the Louisiana Territory from France. At first, in 1801, President Jefferson only wanted to purchase land at the mouth of the Mississippi River where the river empties into the Gulf of Mexico. However, since the French government would only sell all of the Louisiana Territory, Jefferson finally decided to buy all the land. This purchase in 1803 doubled the size of the United States to include most of the central plains west of the Mississippi River to the Rocky Mountains.

The famous expedition of exploration up the Missouri began in 1804. However, preparation for the journey began in the East a few years before. In 1802 Jefferson selected Meriwether Lewis to lead an expedition. During the next two years preparations continued and William Clark was made co-captain. Lewis studied to improve his scientific skills and knowledge with some of the most educated men in their fields. Decisions on what to bring and how much were made. Goods made or purchased at Philadelphia and Harpers Ferry were transported to the Ohio River. The large keelboat was built in Pittsburgh. Selection of the crew began in 1803 when Lewis left Pittsburgh on the trip down the Ohio. Stops were made at various places including Wheeling, Cincinnati, the Falls of the Ohio, Fort Massac, and Fort Kaskaskia before they finally reached the base camp at Wood River across from the mouth of the Missouri River.

The 1804-6 trail out and back that was explored by Lewis and Clark was about eight thousand miles long. It took them up the Missouri River Valley, through vast grasslands called prairies. They used boats for most of the journey up the river. When they came to the Rocky Mountains they had to walk or ride horses over them. They used Indian trails, such as Nez Perce Trail, now called the Lolo Trail. Finally, after crossing the mountains they again came to other rivers and followed them down to the Pacific Ocean. The following year they began their return voyage home to Missouri. The journey lasted twenty-eight months. Since it took more than two years, some people in the East thought that they were lost, captured or dead.

The Corps of Discovery was the name given to the people who traveled with Lewis and Clark on their voyage of discovery. They were to explore and map the region, look for a water route to the Pacific Ocean, make friends with all the Indians, record information about the plants and animals, and look for pre-historic mammoths. There were soldiers, trappers and traders, hearty men who had a desire for adventure. In addition, there were other special travelers. One was York, Clark's Afro-American slave. Another traveler who joined them was Sacagawea, a teen-aged Indian girl. A large Newfoundland dog named Seaman also accompanied the expedition.

They usually traveled about fifteen to twenty miles a day on the journey west. On some days they would only go a few miles. Snags, strong currents, rapids, and waterfalls made navigating the rivers difficult. Also, some mountains were so steep and high it was difficult to cross them.

Very few pioneers used the same route opened by Lewis and Clark. The trail over the mountains was too difficult and wagons could not be easily used. Therefore, when the pioneers started heading west with their wagons they looked for an easier route. The route that the pioneers used came to be called the Oregon-California Trail.

There is a map in the middle of this book. It shows the Louisiana Purchase and the locations of some of the sites and forts that Lewis and Clark saw, visited, or built. Their journey to the Pacific started from Camp Wood at Wood River, Illinois, near St. Louis, Missouri. For most of the journey they followed the Missouri River, then crossed the Rocky Mountains and finally followed the Columbia River until it flowed into the Pacific Ocean.

As you read through this book you will learn many things about the Lewis and Clark Trail and the places associated with it. You will learn about some of the people who traveled on it and the goods they brought along. You will see some drawings of the sights they saw. There are some fun activities and puzzles to do. There is also a game to play, as well as a project to complete. We hope you will enjoy learning about Lewis and Clark this way!

GOOD LUCK!!   Jan & Bill

THE STORY OF MERIWETHER LEWIS

Meriwether Lewis was born at Locust Hill, near Charlottesville, Virginia in 1774. Lewis became the leader of the Corps of Discovery that explored the Louisiana Territory. Lewis had served as a Captain in the army. He was an educated man who loved hunting and exploring the outdoors. These traits were to play an important role when he explored the West. Lewis was also a friend and neighbor of Thomas Jefferson who lived at Monticello. Later, when Jefferson became President, Lewis served as his private secretary. Because of Lewis's knowledge of the outdoors and Indians, his military training, and his loyalty and trustworthiness, President Thomas Jefferson selected him to be the leader of the group that explored the Louisiana Territory. Before he left, Lewis joined the American Philosophical Society in Philadelphia. He continued his studies of medicine, plants, animals, the earth, the stars and the planets, all studies important for his journey. Lewis died in 1809 a few years after he returned.

Lewis was tall and slender, but strong. He had dark hair.

Copy this small drawing of Meriwether Lewis onto the larger empty grid, square by square. When you are done, you will have a larger drawing of him.

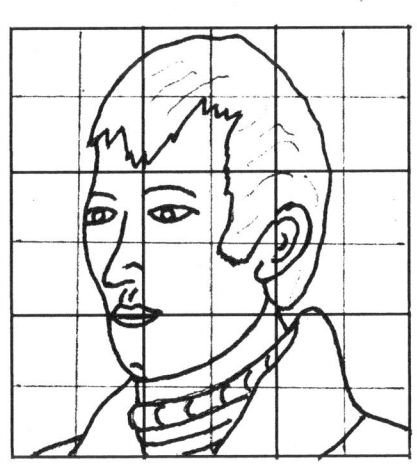

THE STORY OF WILLIAM CLARK

William Clark was born in Virginia in 1770. He received a good education as a young boy, was knowledgeable about the outdoors, and skilled in sketching. All these traits were to be useful to Clark later when he explored the Louisiana Territory. Clark met Lewis when they were both serving in the army. There they became good friends. Later when men were being selected to explore the Louisiana Territory Lewis picked his good friend Clark to share the command. During their explorations one of Clark's jobs was to sketch the different plants and animals they found. After their expedition was over Clark made his home and raised his family in St. Louis, Missouri, on lands now occupied by the Jefferson National Expansion Memorial and Gateway Arch. Clark remained interested in the West and in the Indian people. Clark died in 1838.

Clark was over six feet tall and had blue eyes and red hair.

Copy this small drawing of William Clark onto the larger empty grid, square by square. When you are done, you will have a larger drawing of him.

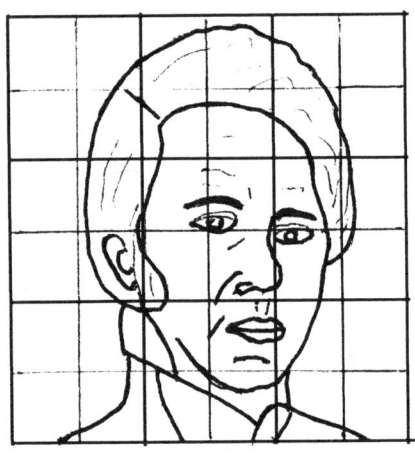

Lewis had the keelboat built in 1803 in Pittsburgh. It was first used to bring supplies down the Ohio River. Lewis stopped to study Indian burial mounds and large bones from pre-historic animals. He also stopped to pick up Captain Clark and other crew members. They arrived at the Wood River near St. Louis and set up their winter camp, called Camp Wood.

On May 14, 1804, the journey of discovery and exploration began. Clark and the Corps of Discovery left Camp Wood and started up the Missouri River. Lewis, who was in St. Louis finishing up business, rode over to St. Charles to join them a few days later. When they left St. Charles they left civilization. They were off into the unknown. They would not return until September 23, 1806. They began with the one large keelboat and two smaller pirogues which were canoe-like boats. One pirogue was red and the other one was white. The keelboat could be sailed, rowed, poled or pulled up river. Their journey would last twenty-eight months, and the party would travel over eight thousand miles. You can draw two pirogues on the river if you wish.

By October, 1804, the Lewis and Clark expedition reached the Mandan Indian village near present-day Bismarck, North Dakota. The Mandans and their neighbors, the Hidatsas, lived in earthen lodges which had wooden frameworks. In the center of each roof was a small hole which served as a chimney for the smoke to go out. In the village there were decorated poles which were used in religious ceremonies. Lewis and Clark decided to remain in the area for the winter. Nearby they built Fort Mandan to live in. Today you can visit a reconstruction of the village and fort. They are located near Washburn, North Dakota.

York, one of the special travelers on the expedition, was Clark's Afro-American slave. York was tall, strong, good looking, and was said to have a good sense of humor. At that time the Indians had never met a black man before and were very interested when they met York.

At the Mandan village Lewis and Clark met a trader called Toussaint Charbonneau. He was married to a sixteen year old Shoshone, Sacagawea. Her name meant "Bird Woman." When she was younger she had been captured in a raid and taken far from her own people. Charbonneau and Sacagawea would both serve as interpreters. Since Sacagawea had lived in the western mountains, she would play a very important role and help point the way west for Lewis and Clark when they came near the Rocky Mountains. That winter Sacagawea had a baby boy, named Jean-Baptiste, who was nicknamed Pomp.

Another special traveler who was part of the Corps of Discovery was Lewis's dog. He was a large black Newfoundland named Seaman. Lewis had purchased Seaman for twenty dollars in the East in 1803 before leaving Pittsburgh. Seaman first met Captain Clark at the Falls of the Ohio River. They became friends. Seaman was very helpful. He was good at retrieving game and also served as a good watchdog. He was especially useful by warning the men whenever a grizzly bear was nearby. Seaman also saved the captains from being trampled by a stampeding buffalo.

When Lewis and Clark wintered at Fort Mandan, the Indians had told them about a series of large waterfalls far to the west on the Missouri River. On July 13, 1805 Lewis and Clark reached the Great Falls of the Missouri River. It was only one of the many natural wonders they encountered. A few miles before reaching one of the large falls Lewis could hear the roar and see the mist of the waterfalls. When he saw the Great Falls he wrote in his journal that they were the "...grandest sight I ever beheld." The falls were about 900 feet wide and 80 feet tall. The Great Falls are a series of five major falls and other minor ones which the expedition had to portage(carry) their boats around. Today, the city of Great Falls, Montana, has grown up there and portions of the falls have been dammed.

One of the important things Lewis and Clark did was to draw the new plants and animals they saw on the journey. They even sent some samples of them back east to President Jefferson to be studied and displayed. They saw buffalo, antelope, beavers, grizzly bears, wolves, snakes, and many different kinds of fish and birds. Many of the plants and animals were unknown to the explorers. On the next few pages are dot to dot drawings of other animals they saw.

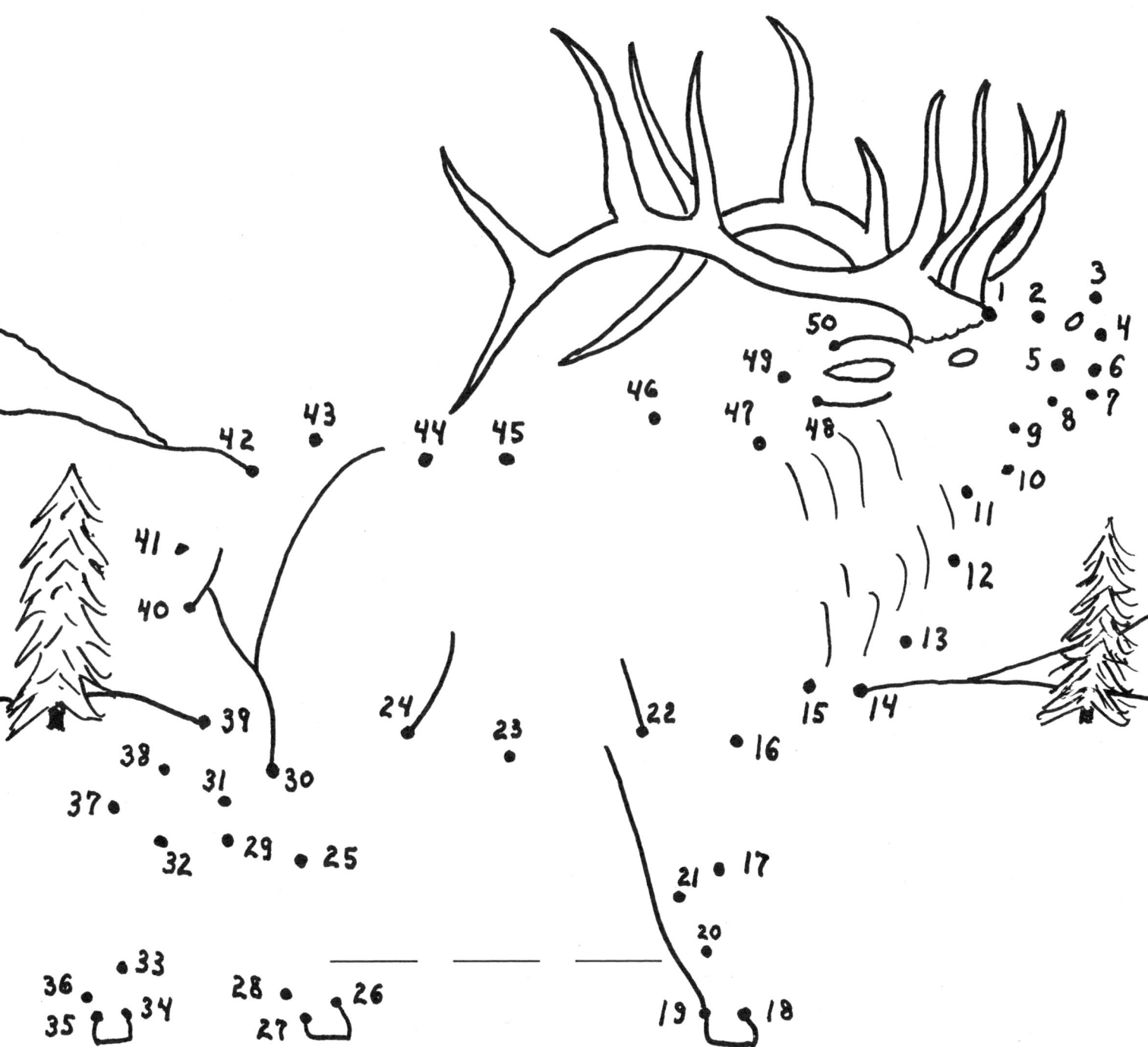

This animal is larger than either a deer or a pronghorn antelope. It was found in large herds on the Great Plains and in the mountains. Today it is rarely seen on the plains, but it is still seen in the mountains. Complete the dot to dots. Write its name in the spaces above.

The members of the Corps of Discovery had sailed, rowed, poled and pulled their boats up the Missouri River as far as they could go. Now they needed a way to get over the Rocky Mountains. When Sacagawea met her own people, the Shoshone, she helped Lewis and Clark trade for this animal. It helped carry them over the mountains on the Lolo Trail in present-day Idaho. What is the animal?

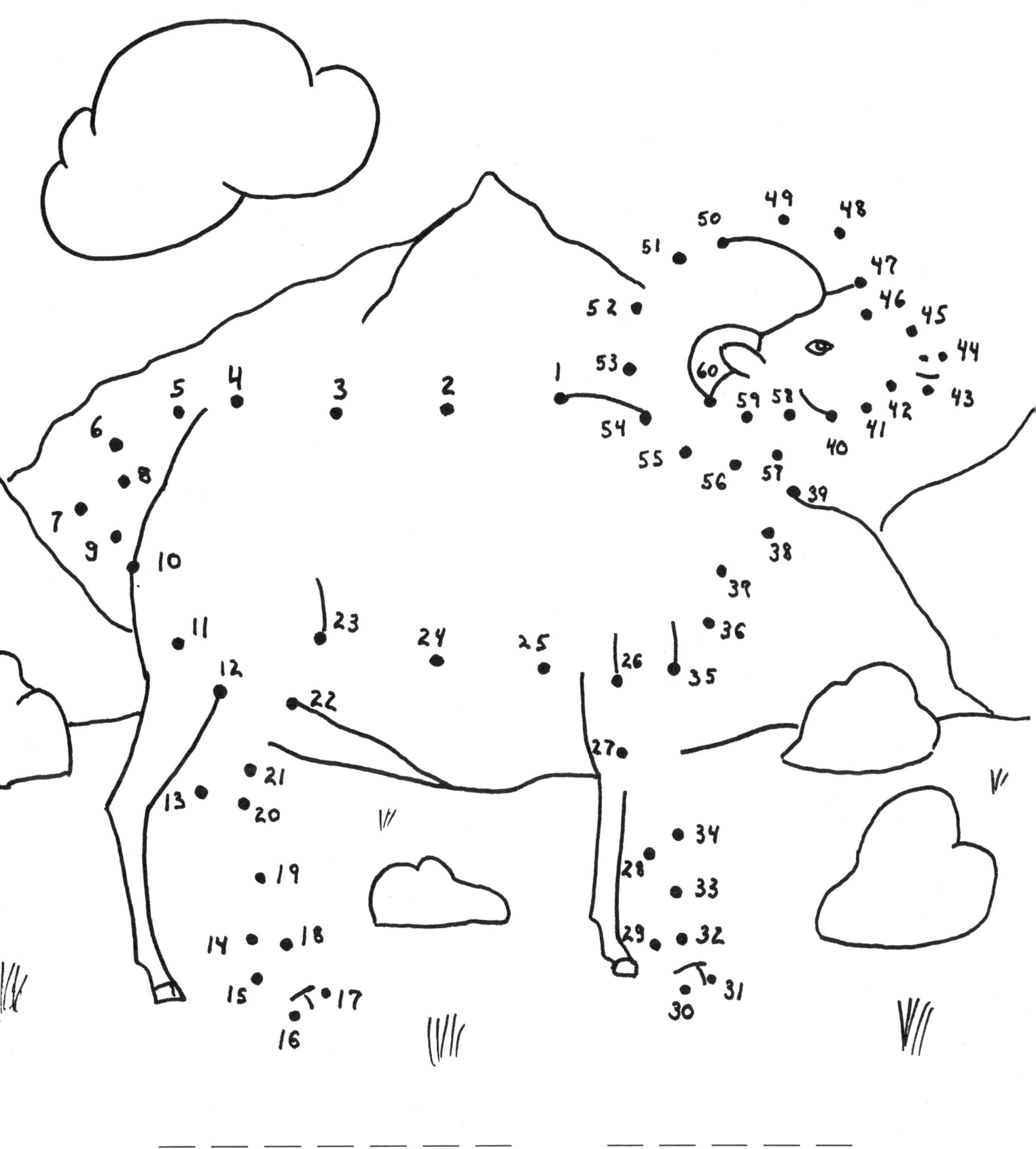

_ _ _ _ _ _ _ _ _ _ _ _

Lewis and Clark saw this animal and hunted it many times when they were crossing the mountains. It has very good footing and large curved horns. Complete the dot to dots. Then write its name in the spaces above.

Once the Corps of Discovery crossed the Rocky Mountains they met the friendly Nez Perce Indians. They obtained food, canoes and information about how to get to the Pacific Ocean from the Nez Perce. They started canoeing down the Clearwater River, then the Snake River and finally came to the Columbia River. One day Clark climbed out of the river valley onto the Columbia plateau. Far off in the distance he saw the Cascade Mountains. However, nearby he saw the smaller rock formation drawn above. What do you think he called the formation? Look carefully at its shape. If you called it "Hat Rock," you are correct. It is located in north central Oregon on the Columbia River in Hat Rock State Park.

The local Indians told Lewis and Clark that there were many dangerous rapids and cascades on the Columbia River before it reached the ocean. After days of canoeing and going through many rapids and cascades the expedition came to a huge dark rock formation on the north side of the river. It is called Beacon Rock. There they noticed signs of the ocean's tidewater. Then they knew they were past the dangers and almost at the Pacific Ocean. Beacon Rock is on the Washington side of the Columbia River.

On November 6, 1805, four days after passing Beacon Rock, Clark wrote in his journal, "Ocean 4,142 miles from the mouth of the Missouri River." Nearby they built Fort Clatsop, named after a local Indian tribe. There they spent the winter of 1805-6. In the spring they began their return journey. Today you can visit a reconstruction of Fort Clatsop, near Astoria, Oregon, and see how Lewis and Clark and the Corps of Discovery lived that winter.

On their return journey Lewis and Clark and the other members of the expedition were able to travel faster since they knew the route. However, once in the mountains they split up to look for an easier way through the mountains. Lewis went farther north, and Clark explored another route south. Along the Yellowstone River Clark came to a tall large rock formation. Clark called the rock formation "Pompy's Tower," after Sacagawea's baby boy Pomp. Clark also carved his own name on it. Today you can still see the rock, only its name is now Pompey's Pillar, and Clark's name is now protected under plastic. It is located east of Billings, Montana.

WORD PUZZLER

President Thomas Jefferson asked Lewis and Clark to meet and make friends with the different Indian tribes that lived in the areas they explored. Jefferson wanted the Indian leaders to be given a medal to wear. Below is a drawing of the medal. One side had a carving of Jefferson on it. The other side which showed two hands shaking had a message carved on it. Use the word puzzler on the next page to find out what the message was. The real size of the medal was much smaller than the drawing below.

WORD PUZZLER

Below are drawings of items associated with trappers, traders, explorers and Indians. Fill in the missing letters next to each picture clue. Then write the letter from each numbered box in the numbered space below. Also write the letters in the drawing on page 18. They will spell the words that were on the medals presented to the Indians.

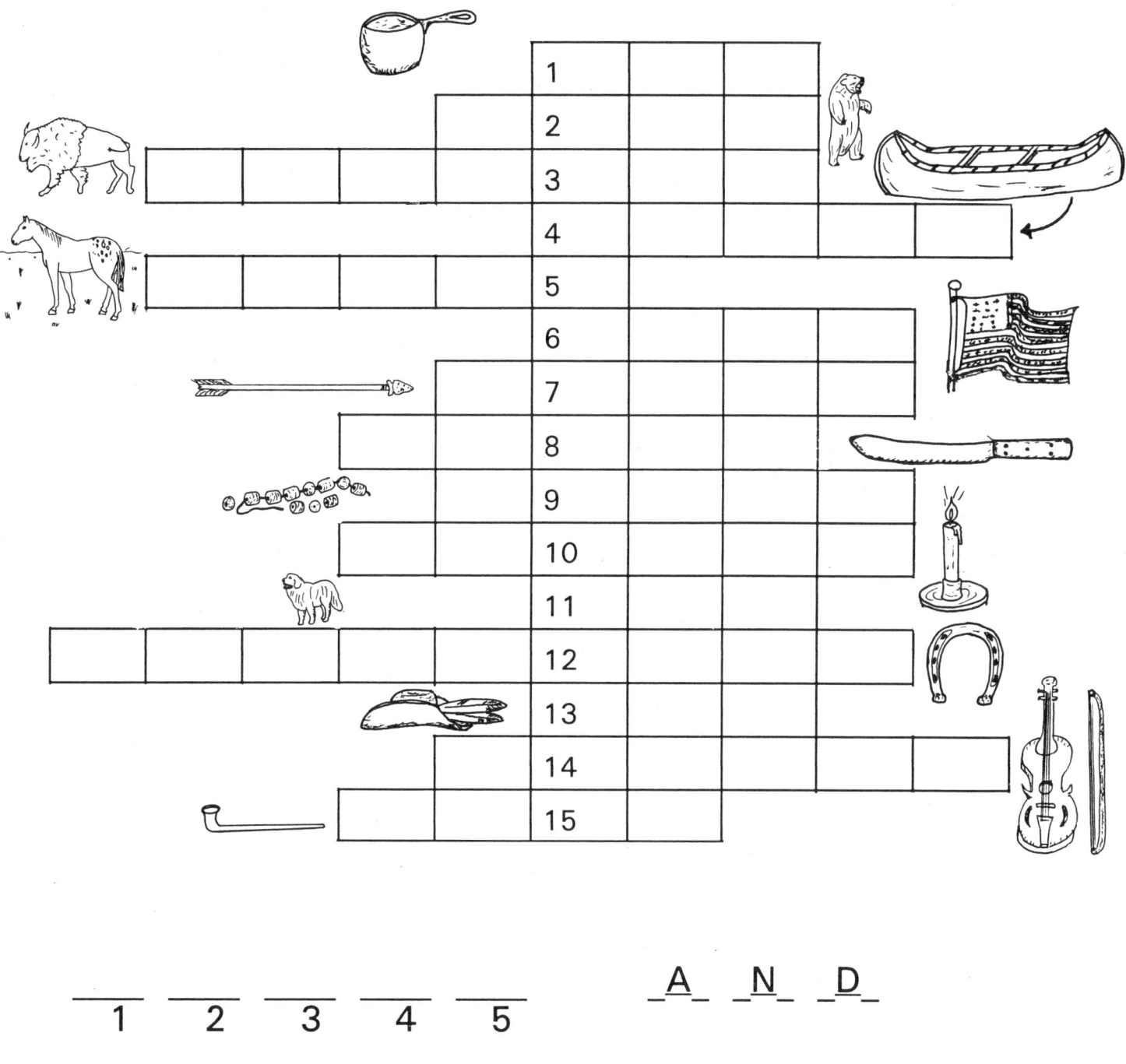

   _ _ _ _ _   _A_ _N_ _D_
   1 2 3 4 5

   _ _ _ _ _ _ _ _ _ _ !
   6 7 8 9 10 11 12 13 14 15

Map of the United States today showing the Louisiana Territory, the 1803 route from Pittsburgh to Wood River, and the 1804-6 Lewis and Clark Trail.

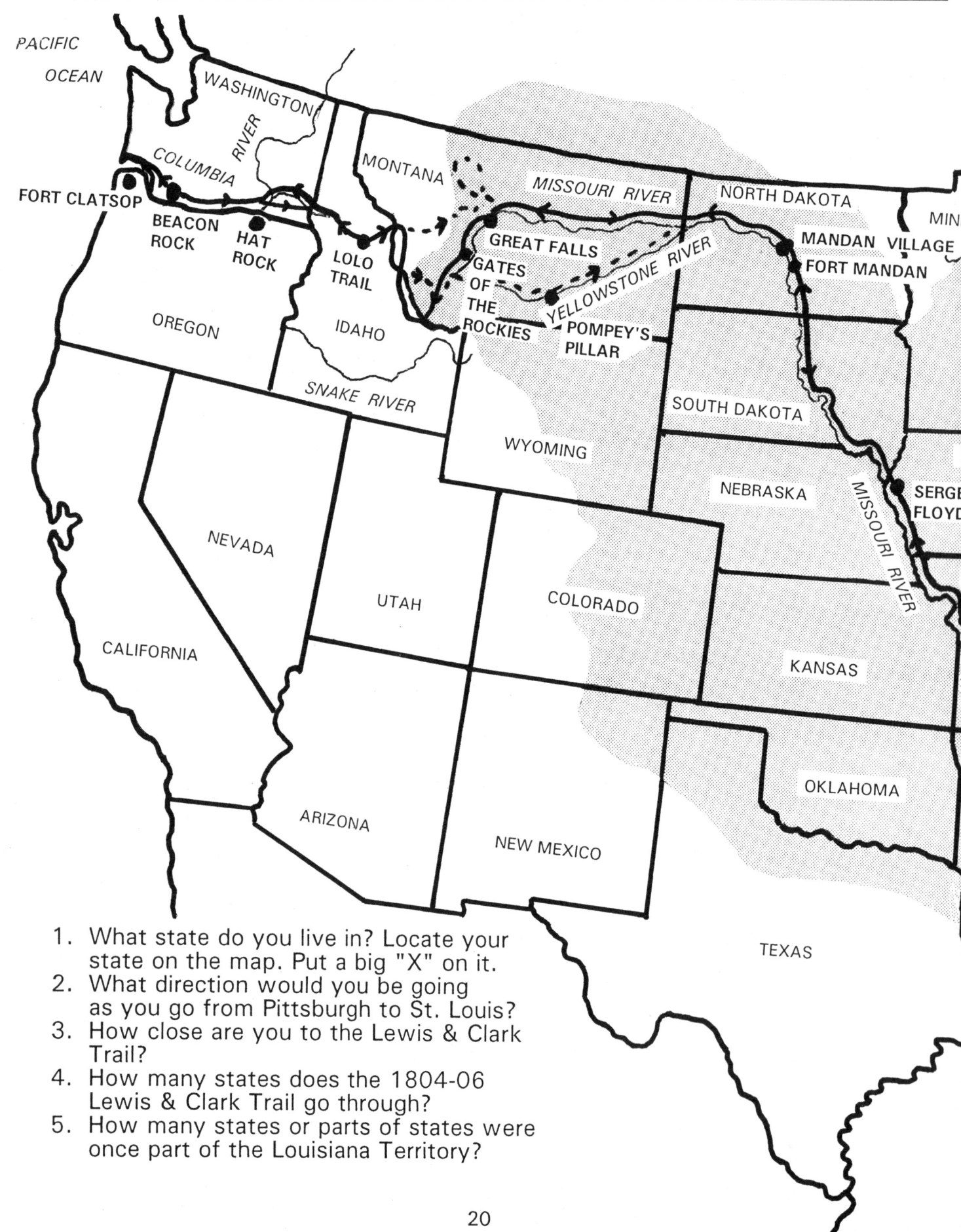

1. What state do you live in? Locate your state on the map. Put a big "X" on it.
2. What direction would you be going as you go from Pittsburgh to St. Louis?
3. How close are you to the Lewis & Clark Trail?
4. How many states does the 1804-06 Lewis & Clark Trail go through?
5. How many states or parts of states were once part of the Louisiana Territory?

Before Jefferson purchased the Louisiana Territory, the western boundary of the United States was the Mississippi River. The shaded area on the map is the Louisiana Territory purchased in 1803. In 1803 Lewis left Pittsburgh and started down the Ohio River. After making many stops to pick up supplies, Captain Clark, and more crew members, the Corps arrived at Camp Wood. Some stops are shown on the map. The 1804-6 Lewis and Clark Trail starts at Camp Wood, Illinois. The route taken down the Ohio River, and then up the Missouri River over to the Columbia River to the Pacific Ocean and back is shown in a solid (←) line. The dash (- - -) lines represent the part of the return journey where Lewis and Clark split up. The dots (●) are the locations of some of the places you read about. The thin (〜) lines represent some of the rivers. Also, part of the route and some rivers used by Lewis and Clark are the borders between states today.

FOODS

Lewis and Clark and the Corps of Discovery did not have all the ready-made frozen and canned foods that we have today. They did bring basic food like salt, flour, salt pork, dried apples, and cornmeal. Two very basic prepared foods that they brought were portable soup and biscuit, also called hardtack. The portable soup was used primarily for emergencies and was probably not very tasty. It is thought to have been prepared by constantly boiling meat and vegetables until the mixture became like a jell or thick paste. Then it was canned.

The Corps of Discovery also relied on fish and meat they obtained from hunting, fishing or trading with the Indians they met. Most of their foods were either cooked or boiled over an open fire. They also dried or jerked some of the meat when they could or used it to make pemmican which was a mixture of crushed meat, fat, and berries. Buffalo meat was a favorite of the men. Some days they had more food then they needed, and at other times they almost starved. Here are some simple recipes you might want to prepare with the help of an adult.

BUFFALO & FISH - On August 23, 1804, Private Joseph Field shot the first of many buffalo that the men would eat. Buffalo is much leaner than beef and each man needed to eat about 9 pounds of meat a day.

Along the Missouri River on August 15, 1804, Clark and 10 men went fishing and caught over 300 fish. The next day Lewis and 12 men caught more than 700 fish, including 167 Northern Pike, hundreds of catfish, both small and large mouth bass, perch and many other types of fish. Later, along the Columbia River they caught and traded for salmon.

Today you can buy some of the same types of fish from a grocery store or you might be able to catch them in a local stream or river. Your parents can also order buffalo meat. Then you can barbecue the buffalo steaks or fry the fish.

HARDTACK or BISCUIT
This food was used by explorers and soldiers on the frontier, sailors on the oceans, and pioneers going west. It was simple to prepare, would keep for a long time, but it was not very tasty. It is made without yeast. It is <u>very</u> <u>hard</u> and was often soaked in a liquid such as water, soup, or coffee before it was eaten.

INGREDIENTS

2 cups flour   1 cup water   fork   cookie sheet

1. Combine water and flour.
2. Knead until smooth.
3. Roll dough flat, 1/4 inch thick.
4. Cut into two or three inch squares using a knife or round shapes using a cookie cutter. You could use a glass or opened can if you don't have a round cookie cutter.
5. Poke holes in each piece of the dough using a fork.
6. Bake on a cookie sheet for about 35 minutes at 400 degrees.

INDIAN BREAD or CORNBREAD
Lewis and Clark's men often recorded that they traded for cornbread made by the Indians. They also noted that it sometimes had berries mixed in, and sometimes even beans, and that it was either made flat or into round balls. The Indians used saskatoons, also called serviceberries. They are similar to blueberries and huckleberries. Currants can also be used as well as most other edible berries and raisins.

INGREDIENTS -

2 cups cornmeal   1/4 - 1/2 cup berries (optional)   1/2 tsp salt
1 tsp baking powder   2 tbsp butter, bacon grease, or shortening   1 cup water or milk

1. Mix dry ingredients in a bowl.
2. Add shortening and enough water to make a smooth dough.
3. Knead the dough.
4. Optional - Add the berries and mix.
5. Pat flat or make into small balls and place into greased 8x8 baking dish, or pour into greased muffin pan.
6. Bake in the oven at 425 degrees for about 30 minutes or until brown. Less time is needed for muffins.

Try it with honey while it is still warm.

  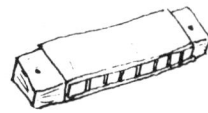

MUSIC

Music was important to the Corps of Discovery. After a day of hard work, the music and songs helped the members relax. It helped them forget the hardships. Not only did they enjoy the music, but the Indians they met and stayed with enjoyed it also. Some men brought harmonicas, tin whistles, tambourines, jaw harps and sounden horns. Pierre Cruzatte even brought his fiddle(violin). Another man was known for dancing upside down on his head or hands, to the amusement of all!

Below is one of the songs that was popular during the time of Lewis and Clark. You may know it. As with many songs, people changed and made up their own words to the music. See if you can too!

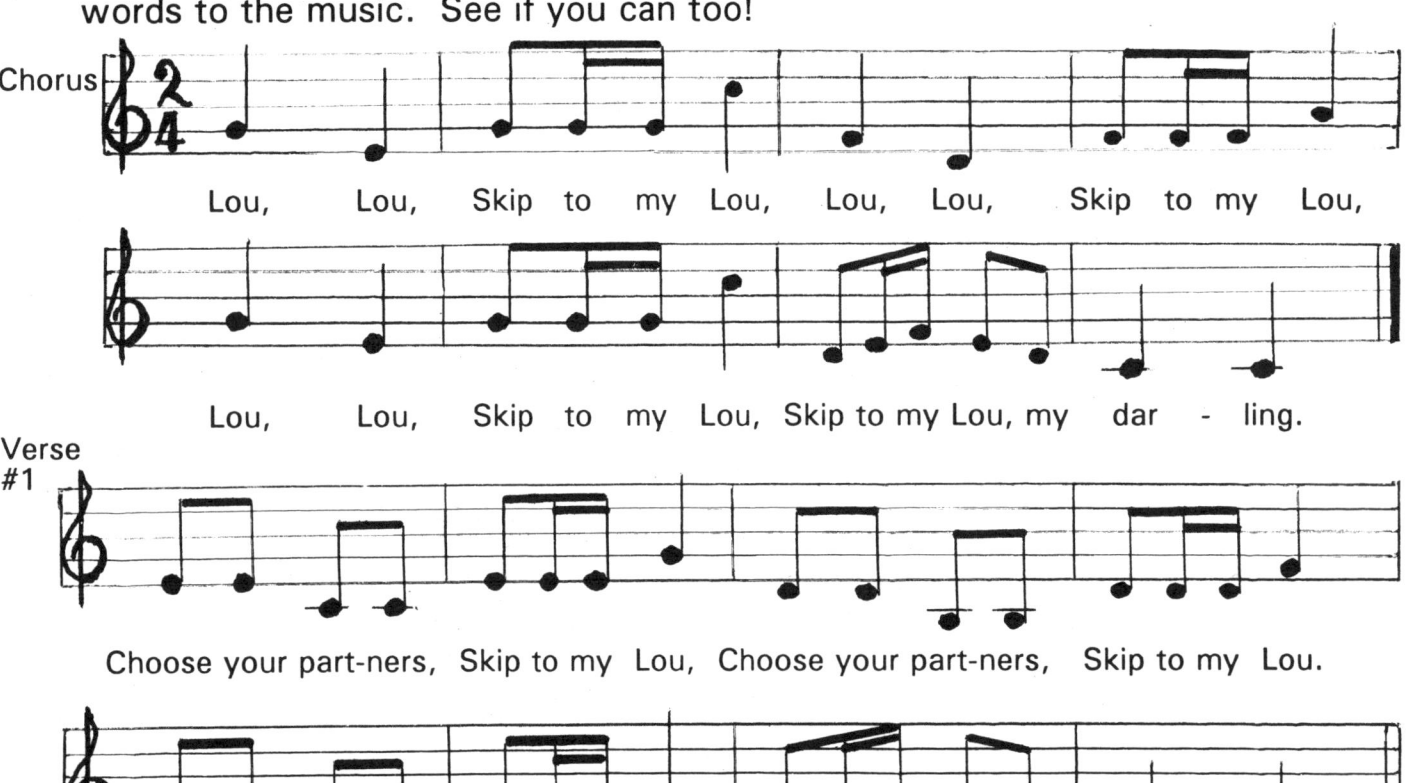

Chorus

Lou, Lou, Skip to my Lou, Lou, Lou, Skip to my Lou,

Lou, Lou, Skip to my Lou, Skip to my Lou, my dar - ling.

Verse #1

Choose your part-ners, Skip to my Lou, Choose your part-ners, Skip to my Lou.

Choose your part-ners, Skip to my Lou, Skip to my Lou, my dar - ling.

Chorus - sing again after each verse.

2. Lost my partner, what'll I do, Lost my partner, what'll I do,
   Lost my partner, what'll I do, Skip to my Lou my darling.

3. I'll get a partner, prettier than you, I'll get a partner, prettier than you,
   I'll get a partner, prettier than you, Skip to my Lou my darling.

4. Cat in the cream jar, what'll I do, Cat in the cream jar, what'll I do,
   Cat in the cream jar, what'll I do, Skip to my Lou my darling.

5. Fly in the sugar bowl, shoo, fly, shoo, Fly in the sugar bowl, Shoo, fly, shoo,
   Fly in the sugar bowl, shoo, fly, shoo, Skip to my Lou my darling.

INDIAN CHILDREN'S GAME

Members of the Corps of Discovery were asked to keep journals. One of those who kept a journal was Sergeant John Ordney. On Saturday, December 15, 1804, he described a game played by the Mandan men. Indian children of various tribes played similar games. Different tribes used different sized hoops and poles. Their games often encouraged the development of skills which they might need later as adult members of their tribes. Below is a description of the Hoop and Pole game. Perhaps you can try to play it with your friends.

Equipment - (See diagrams)
  Hoop - Size - diameter varies from about 4 inches to 2 1/2 feet.
    Material - made out of wood, leather, clay or stone.
    Sometimes the hoop is left open, but when using the larger hoops the Indians often made a netting with a opening in the center.
  Pole - Length - varies from about 2 feet to about 6 feet.
    Material - straight stick of wood.
    Sometimes the pole would have a fork or wooden barbs on it.

The game was played with two teams. A player from each team would be paired with the other. Both members would start running. The player having the hoop would throw or roll the hoop. Each player would then try to throw his pole or stick at the hoop. The object of the game was to have the stick pass through the center or "heart" of the hoop which resulted in the highest points. If the stick caught the hoop on the first barbs or not in the center hole fewer points were awarded. Indian villages often had game fields that were about 50 yards long, much like the football, baseball or soccer fields we have today.

American Children's Game

Early American children also played Hoop and Stick games. The hoop was about three feet in diameter and the stick was about one foot long. Children would race each other while rolling their hoops with the stick. Sometimes the hoop would be used in place of a jump rope and at other times children would swing the hoop around their waist as happened during the Hula Hoop craze of the 1950s.

DANGERS

Lewis and Clark and the Corps of Discovery had to overcome many dangers and obstacles that threatened them. Only one person died during the whole journey, Sergeant Charles Floyd, who became sick. His grave is near Sioux City, Iowa. Find a safe path for the expedition to take so they will avoid the other dangers shown below. Draw a line to show the safe route.

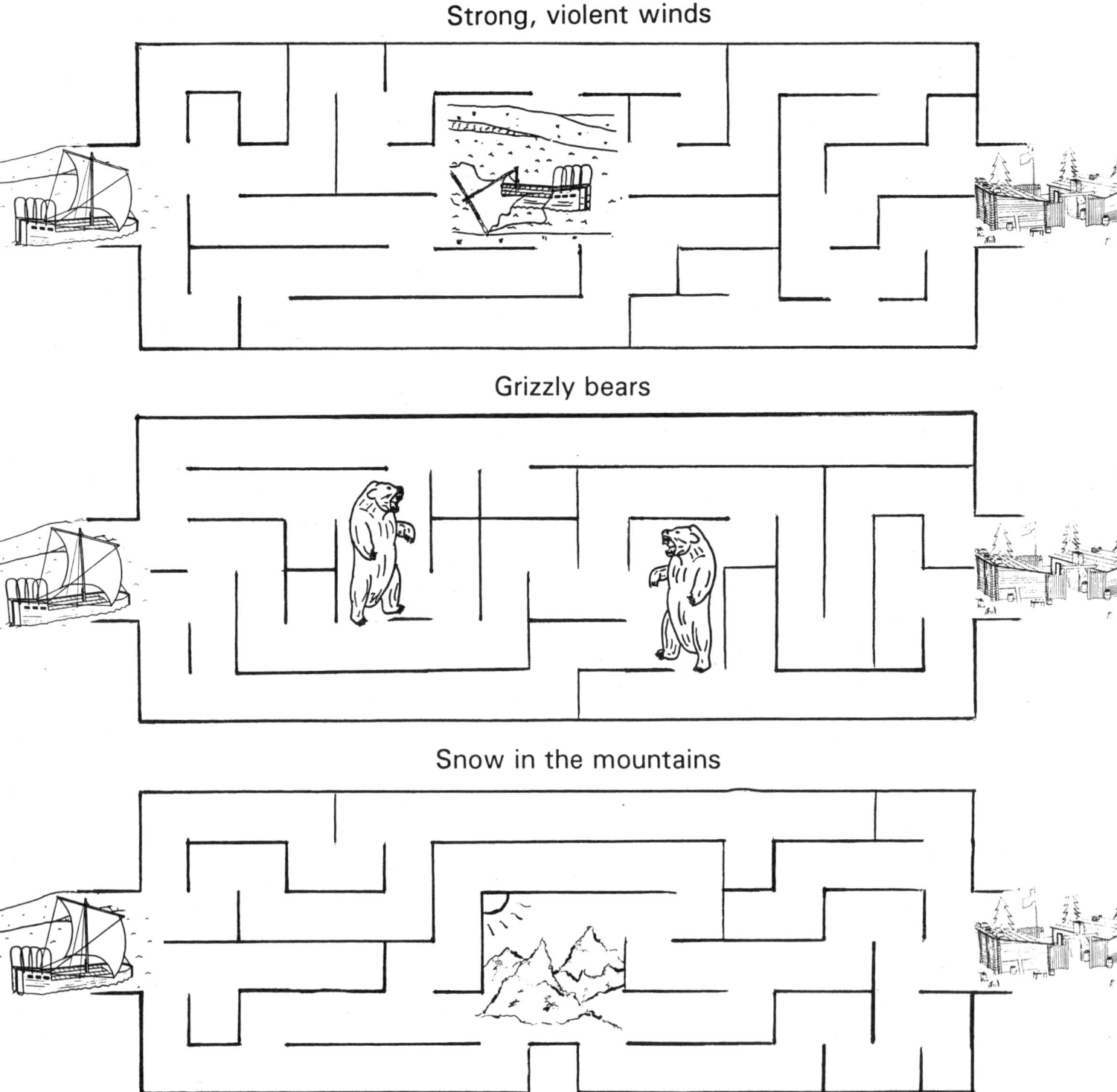

What were some of the other dangers or obstacles they faced?

Help Lewis and Clark and the Corps of Discovery find their way to the Pacific Ocean. Draw a path for them to follow. After leaving Camp Wood on the keelboat go to the Mandan Village. Then continue on to the Lolo Trail through the mountains and finally on to the Pacific Ocean where they built Fort Clatsop.

Camp Wood, Illinois (Start here)

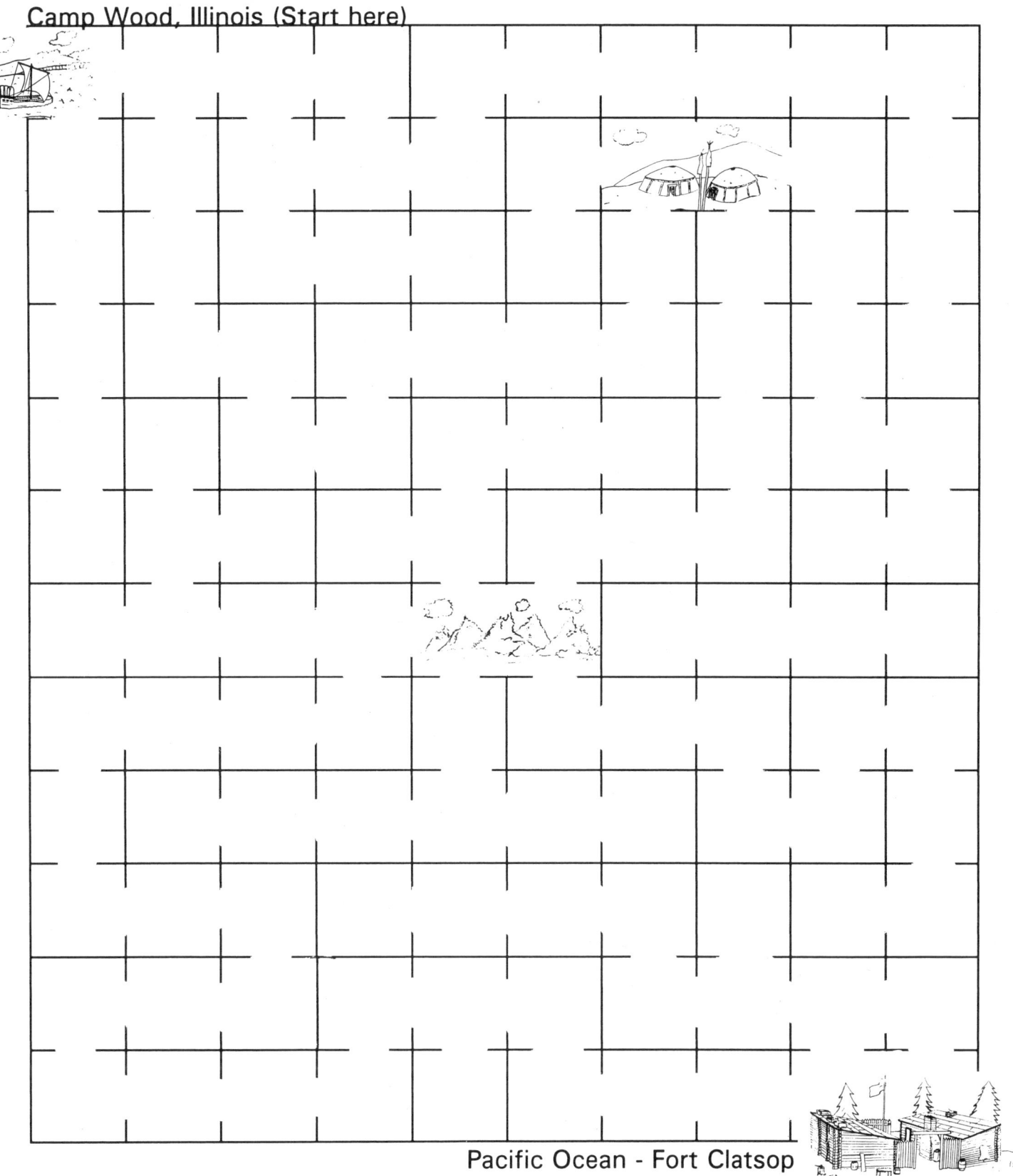

Pacific Ocean - Fort Clatsop

WHAT IS MISSING?

Study the top drawing which shows Fort Mandan where Lewis and Clark spent the winter of 1804-5.
Ten things are missing in the bottom drawing.
Do you know what they are? Add them to the bottom drawing.

CAN YOU FIND THE HIDDEN ITEMS?

A few days after leaving the Great Falls, the Corps of Discovery camped on a sandy beach near the "Gates of the Rocky Mountains." Find the trading items and equipment so they can pack their canoes and continue their journey through the Missouri River canyon.

Here are the hidden items that you are to find in the drawing.

Thimble	Knife	Ax	Pot
Fish hook	Cloth	Needle	Telescope
Comb	Scissors	Thread	Powder horn
String of beads			

WEST WITH LEWIS AND CLARK

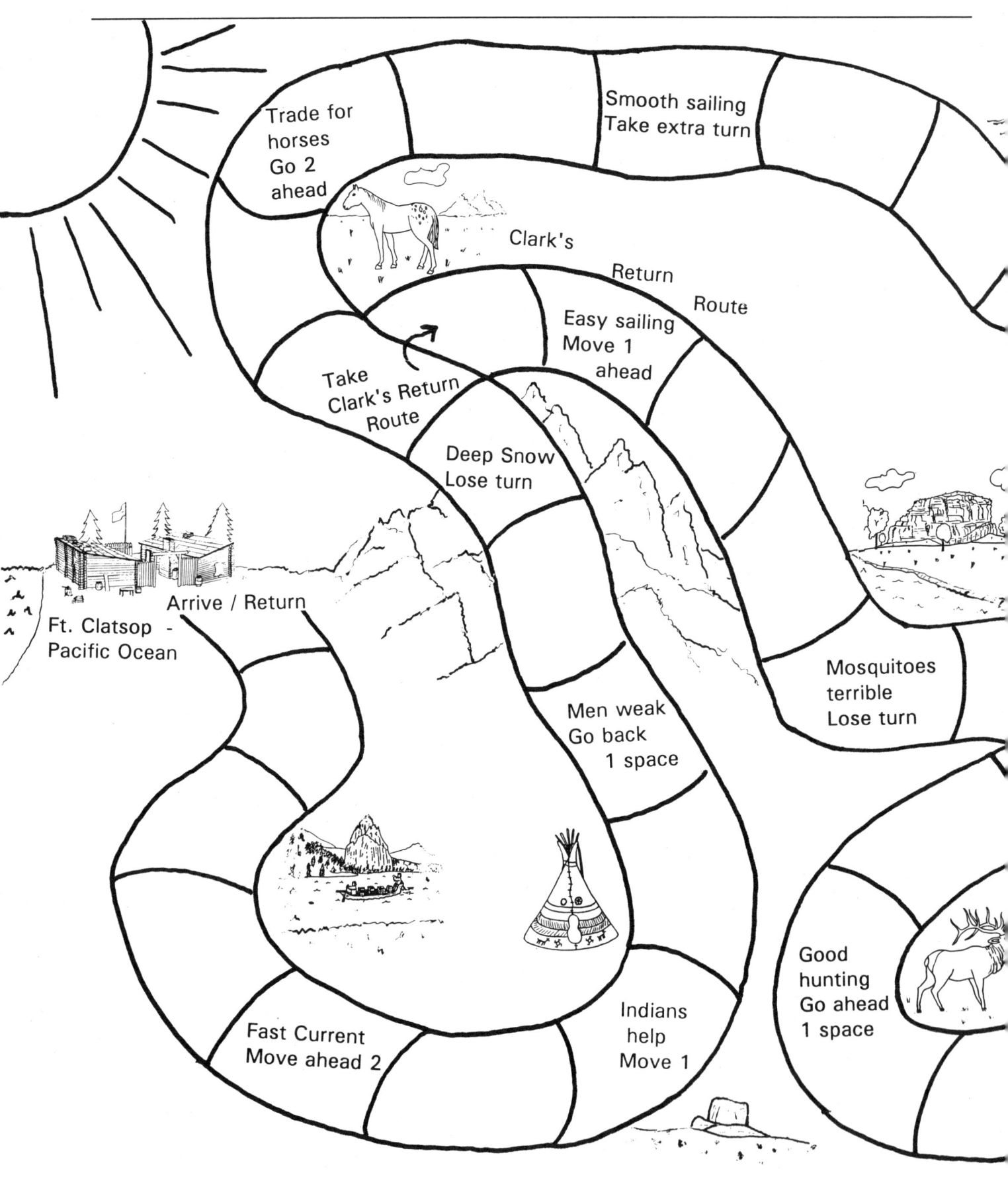

INSTRUCTIONS:

1. Use different coins as markers for each player.
2. Shake and drop three coins.
3. Advance one space for each head thrown.
4. Be sure to follow the instructions on the marked spaces.
5. The first player to reach the Pacific and return to Wood River wins.

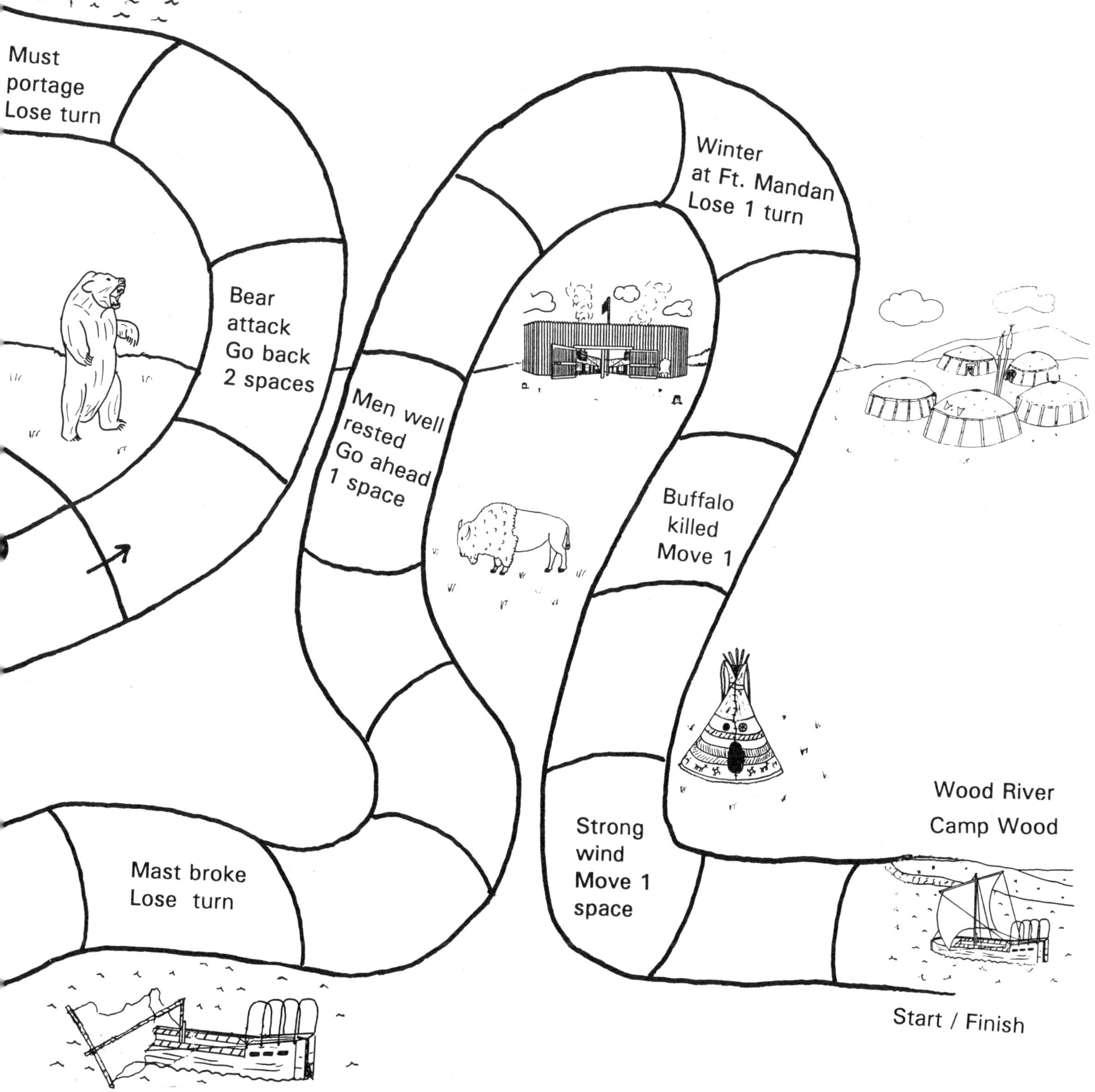

Must portage Lose turn

Bear attack Go back 2 spaces

Winter at Ft. Mandan Lose 1 turn

Men well rested Go ahead 1 space

Buffalo killed Move 1

Mast broke Lose turn

Strong wind Move 1 space

Wood River Camp Wood

Start / Finish

31

Two pictures in each row are exactly the same. Circle them.

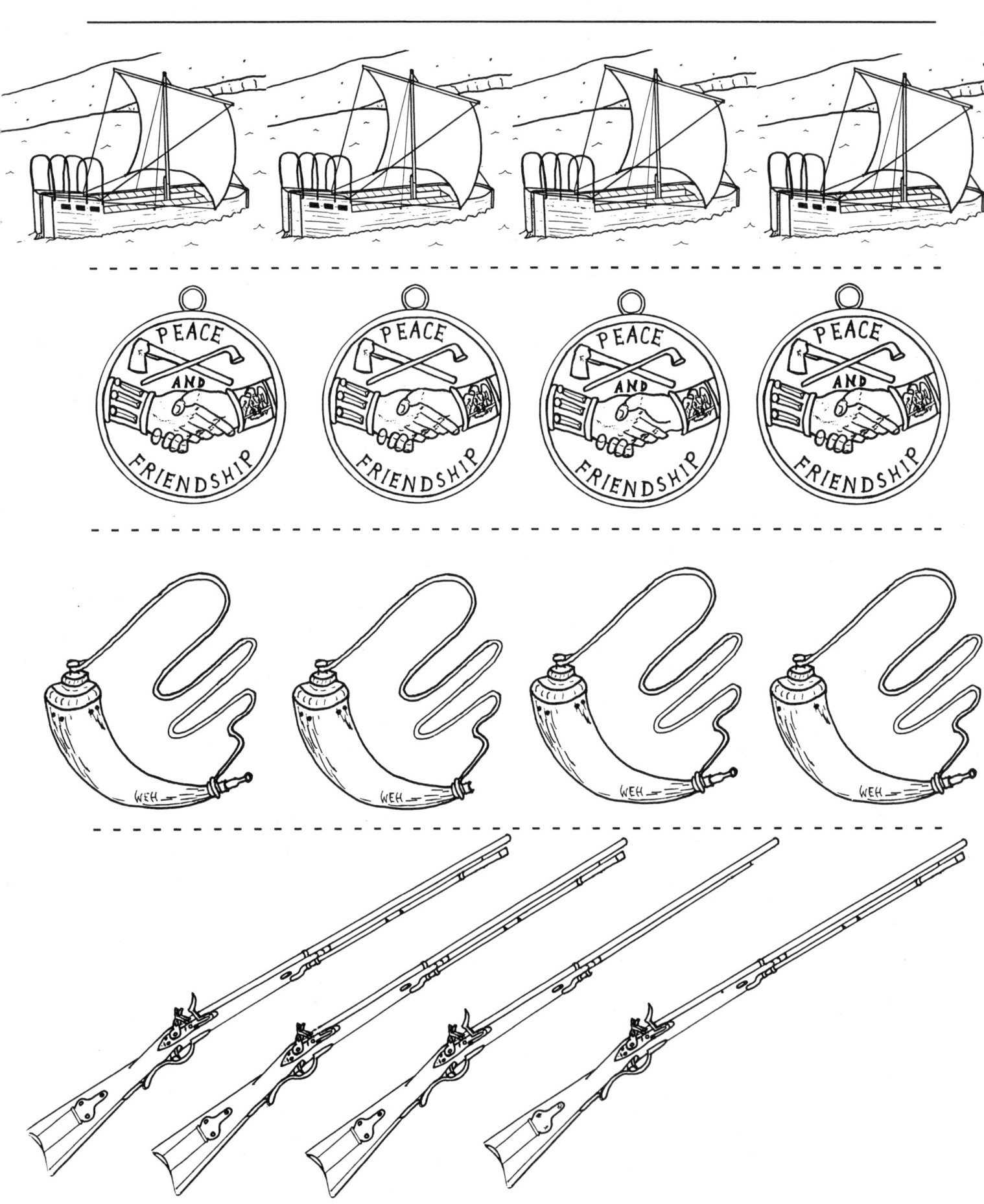

32

HOW MANY CAN YOU MAKE?

How many words you can make using the letters in these four items below?

LEWIS / CLARK

FORT CLATSOP

SACAGAWEA

MISSOURI RIVER

If you work by yourself, see how many you can make. If you and a friend play, see who can be the first to find at least eight words for each section.

CAN YOU FIND IT?

Read the story below. It is about an incident that happened in the very early morning of May 29, 1805. Then find the underlined words in the puzzle below.

Seaman Saves the Camp

After a long hard day of pulling the boats up the Missouri River Lewis and Clark and their party set up camp on the shore of the river. A large herd of buffalo was grazing on the opposite shore, but the river was wide and the people felt safe. After eating supper everybody went to sleep in their tents or around the campfire. In the darkness of the night the guard did not see the big bull buffalo swimming across the river. When it got to the shore the buffalo jumped over one of the boats and ran right towards the men sleeping around the campfire. Luckily it missed all the men who were now awakened. Now the bull was headed right towards Lewis's tent where he was sleeping. The men tried to scare the bull, but it paid no attention to them. Just as it was about to trample the tent Seaman, Lewis's dog, ran after the buffalo barking ferociously. He scared the buffalo away saving Lewis and the other men.

```
B  A  S  W  I  M  M  I  N  G  K  C  T
U  M  B  L  E  W  I  S  R  O  R  A  R
F  C  A  M  P  F  I  S  E  C  A  M  A
F  L  R  T  E  N  T  E  S  D  L  P  M
O  A  K  B  U  F  F  A  L  O  C  F  P
L  N  I  G  H  T  D  M  T  G  U  I  L
A  K  N  O  I  B  O  A  T  S  O  R  E
C  O  G  R  A  Z  I  N  G  E  B  E  I
```

YESTERDAY AND TODAY - A CAMPING TRIP

Times have changed since Lewis and Clark traveled west. Their expedition was like a long camping trip. Below are a list of items. Decide where the items belong, and then print them in the spaces in the diagram.

camera	nylon jacket	buffalo robe
blanket	drawing pad	tent
buckskin jacket	radio	cooler
CD player	fishing tackle	cell phone
telescope	video game	matches
suitcase	quill pen	felt tip pen
fiddle	compass	case of soda
barrel of flour	flint & steel	hardtack
		powder horn

Taken by:

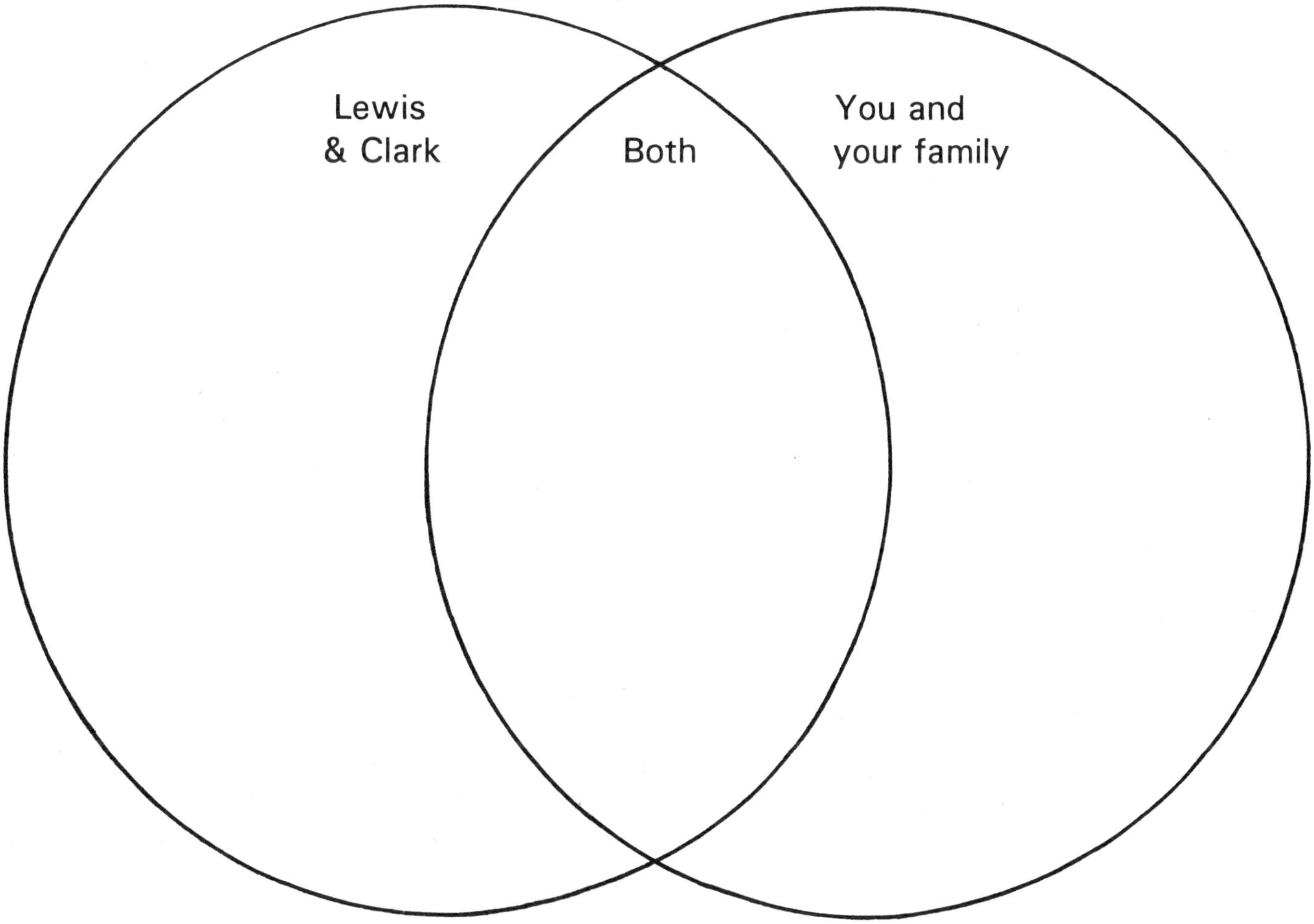

Lewis & Clark   Both   You and your family

CROSSWORD PUZZLE

Write the letters of the words in the spaces to solve the crossword puzzle.

ACROSS
1. Type of boat used by Lewis & Clark.
2. Large horned animal used for food & clothing.
3. Major river in Louisiana Territory.
4. Bird Woman's name.
5. City in which Lewis & Clark's boat was built.

DOWN
6. Lewis & Clark traveled to the (?) Ocean.
7. Seaman was Lewis's (?).
8. Type of animal known as a "Grizzly"
9. Man selected by President Jefferson to lead the expedition.
10. Fort built in 1804.

HOW TO BUILD A KEELBOAT

Materials:
Shoebox - long narrow one is best.
One pencil or dowel rod - for the mast
Two pieces of white paper, 8 1/2 x 11 - to be trimmed as needed for the sail & cover
Scotch tape, glue, scissors
Markers, tempera paints & brush, or crayons - blacks, brown, tan or similar colors
Ruler

Instructions: Ask an adult to help you as needed.

1. Remove the top from the bottom. Set the top aside. It will be used later.

2. Measure the side - length of the shoebox. Divide the side into 4 parts. Mark as shown in the Diagram A below. The 1/4 at one end will be the bow, and the 1/4 at the other end will be the cabin.

3. Measure the height of the shoebox. Divide it into 3 parts. Mark as shown in the Diagram A.

4. Now repeat the same sets of instructions for #3 and #4 on the other long side of the shoebox. Be sure that the cabin end matches the other side.

5. Using the scissors, now make the cuts 1, 2, 3, 4, & 5 on both sides of the shoebox - Diagram A.

6. The bow end of the shoebox can be cut off completely.

7. Turn the shoebox upside down so you are looking at the bottom as in Diagram B. Measure the width of the shoebox and divide it in two as shown in the diagram.

8. Using the scissors, make cuts 6 & 7 to form a point for the bow of the boat. Discard the extra material. See Diagram B. You may have to trim the bow later.

9. In the center half of the both side sections draw black lines one inch apart on the top two-thirds. These will be painted later. See Diagram A.

HOW TO BUILD A KEELBOAT

DIAGRAM A – Side view of shoebox

Fold lines - - - - -
Cut lines ▬▬
Discard ✗✗✗

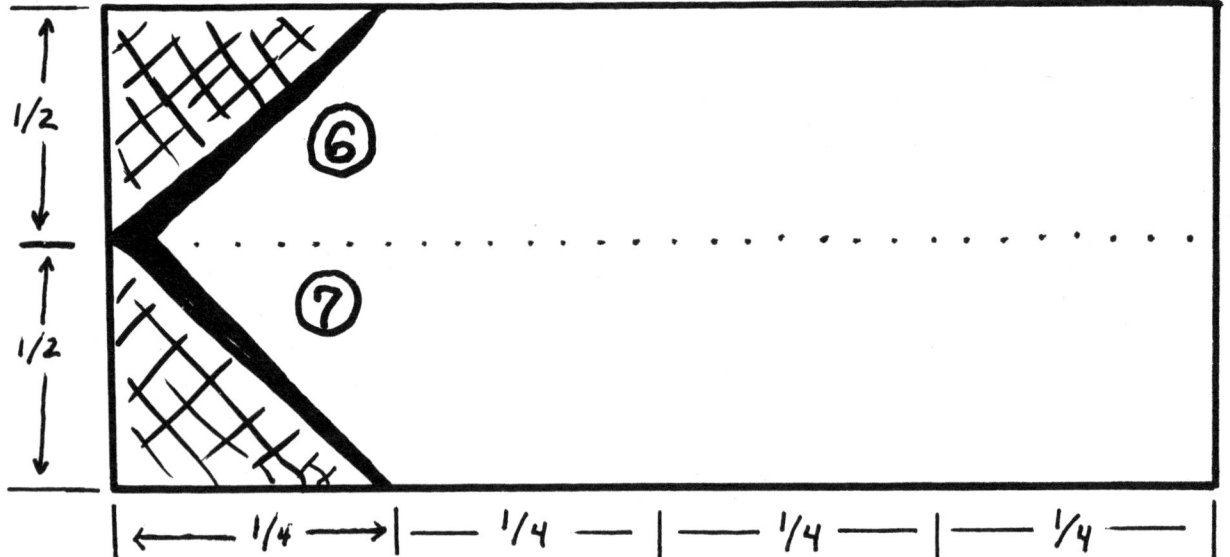

DIAGRAM B – Bottom

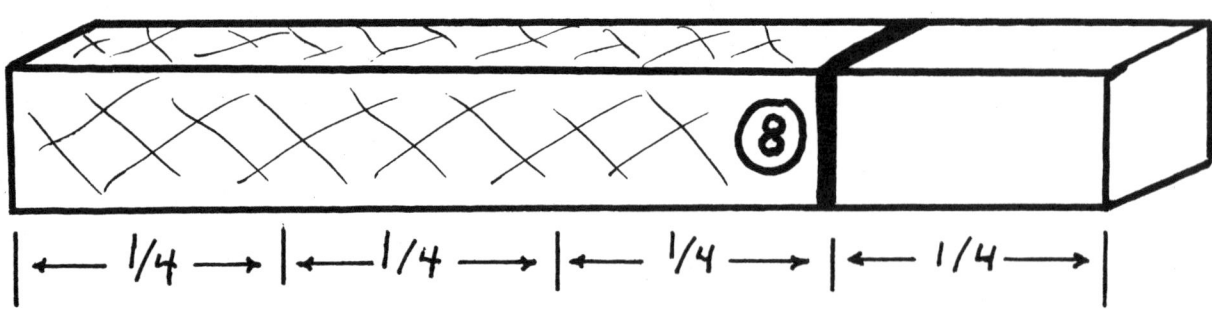

DIAGRAM C – Box top

10. Now make all the folds in order, A, B, C, and then D. Folds A, B and D are 90 degrees. Fold C is about 45 degrees. Be sure to do both sides of the shoebox. You will have to trim off the extra material to have the bow look proper - pointed at the front and square at the back. See Diagram A.

11. Use the tape to hold the pieces in place.

12. Now take the top. Divide it into quarters. Cut one quarter section. This will serve as the top for the cabin. It will slide on the cabin end of the shoebox. The end of the top piece you just cut will cover the open inside of the cabin. Tape or glue the piece in place. See Diagram C, #8.

13. Paint or color the keelboat brown, tan or gray. You may want to paint or color thin black or brown lines on the boat to make it look like wooden boards. You can also paint windows on the cabin as shown below. See Diagram D.

14. Use the pencil to put a hole in the top of the bow. Use the pencil or dowel rod to serve as a mast. Use one piece of white paper for the sail. Put two holes near each end of the paper and slide it on the mast. See diagram D. You may have to tape the mast to the bottom to hold it straight up.

15. Using the second piece of paper, cut it lengthwise to be as wide as the cabin. Glue or tape the paper to form a cover for the top of the cabin area. See Diagram D.

DIAGRAM D

If you or your friends or your parents are interested in learning more about some of the other historic trail related organizations, their names and addresses are listed below. They can all provide you with more information and are fun to join. In addition to the national organizations listed each have state or regional associations you can join. Some associations even have websites.

Join one or join them all!!

Oregon-California Trails Association (OCTA)
524 South Osage Street
P.O.Box 1019
Independence, MO 64051-0519
(816) 252-2276

Santa Fe Trail Association
Santa Fe Tail Center
RR3
Larned, KS 67550
(316) 285-2052

Mormon Trail Association
300 Rio Grande
Salt Lake City, UT 84101-1182

National Pony Express Association
P.O. Box 236
Pollock Pines, CA 95726
www.xphomestation.com/npea

Pony Express Trail Association
139 San Antonio Way
Sacramento, CA 95819
916-456-7404

Manufactured by Thomson-Shore, Dexter, MI (USA); RMA564LS280, December, 2009